BRIAN TRACY'S

Little Silver Book of
PROSPERITY

BRIAN TRACY'S

Little Silver Book of

PROSPERITY

BARNES
&NOBLE
BOOKS
NEW YORK

This edition published by Barnes & Noble, Inc.
by arrangement with Nightingale-Conant Corp.

1995 © Nightingale-Conant Corporation

ISBN 1-56619-862-3

Book design by Rocket Design, James Sarfati

Printed and bound in the United States of America

2 4 6 8 10 M 9 7 5 3 1

ABOUT THE AUTHOR

*A*s the author-narrator of the best-selling audiocassette programs *The Psychology of Achievement* and *The Psychology of Success*, and author of the book *Maximum Achievement*, Brian Tracy is recognized as one of America's leading authorities on the development of human potential and personal effectiveness. He addresses thousands of men and women each year from companies including McDonnell Douglas,

IBM, and Arthur Andersen, bringing his unique perspective to crucial areas of business management such as leadership, goals and strategy, creativity, and success psychology. The trademark of his presentations involves a combination of dynamic storytelling, humor, and concrete ideas easily grasped and implemented. Tracy's human resource company, Brian Tracy International, based in San Diego, has affiliates all over America and in thirty-one countries worldwide.

BRIAN TRACY QUOTATIONS

*E*very great human achievement
is preceded by extended periods of dedicated,
concentrated effort.

*W*e have a mental block inside us that stops us from earning more than we think we are worth. If we want to earn more in reality, we have to upgrade our self-concept.

The day that you stop learning is the day that you start decreasing your rewards and start suffering from frustration and lower levels of satisfaction.

*Y*our choice of people to associate with,
both personally and business-wise,
is one of the most important choices you make.
If you associate with turkeys,
you will never fly with the eagles.

The key to success is to develop
a winning edge.

You can never earn in the outside world
more than you earn in your own mind.

The difference between the top performers and the average or mediocre performers is not a great, massive difference. It is just a tiny difference because the top performers do things just a tiny bit better each day and it adds up to an enormous quantum difference.

*W*hen you develop yourself to the point where your belief in yourself is so strong that you know you can accomplish anything you put your mind to, your future will be unlimited.

*I*f you develop the quality of unshakable self-confidence, your whole world will be different.

*T*he more you like yourself, the better you perform in everything that you do.

With greater confidence in yourself and your abilities, you will set bigger goals and make bigger plans and commit yourself to achieving objectives that today you only dream about.

The biggest mistake we could ever make in our lives is to think we work for anybody but ourselves.

If you spend 30 minutes reading every morning, your whole day is set off right.

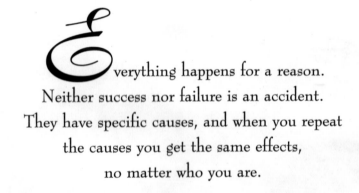

$\mathcal{E}$verything happens for a reason.
Neither success nor failure is an accident.
They have specific causes, and when you repeat
the causes you get the same effects,
no matter who you are.

$\mathscr{A}$lways accept yourself as self-employed and look upon every single thing you accomplish or don't accomplish as your own responsibility.

*Y*ou are where you are and what you are because of the thoughts that you have allowed to preoccupy your mind.

*A*nything that you think about long enough and hard enough eventually becomes a part of your mental processes, exerting its force on your attitudes and your behavior.

*E*verything people experience
in their outer life corresponds exactly to something
that is going on in their inner life.

*R*ecognize that it is natural and normal to fear rejection. The only thing wrong with it is if you allow the fear to dominate you so that it holds you back from fulfilling your potential in your business.

*W*inners are always looking for
a way to deal with the challenges that they face,
and losers are always making excuses
to avoid dealing with challenges.

*T*he solution to the fear
of rejection is to do the thing you fear.
Then the death of fear is certain.

*G*o to bed early and get a good night's sleep
so you feel great in the morning
and have resilience.

19

A truly honest person realizes
that there is no such thing as something for nothing.
There is no easy way to be successful.

When you set a goal,
you program it into the subconscious;
then the subconscious takes on a power of its own
and starts moving you rapidly toward its goal.

$\mathcal{T}$he more you know about yourself,
the more you accept yourself as a valuable
and worthwhile person. The real aim in personality
development is to reach the point where
you accept yourself unconditionally.

*A*ccept that occasionally you are going to run into people that you don't hit it off with. It isn't that either one of you is better or worse, it just means that you are different.

It is very hard for people to resist someone who is listening to them closely, nodding and smiling and showing obvious interest in what they have to say.

The smartest thing that a person can do is to persistently think the thoughts that are consistent with the kind of person he or she would like to be.

*S*uccessful people tend to become more successful because they are always thinking about their successes.

True happiness and success come
from living your life in harmony with
the laws that govern your being.

$\mathcal{L}$iving in truth means that
you never stay in a situation that makes you unhappy
or that you feel is wrong for you for any reason.

The real foundation of self-confidence is living a life consistent with your innermost values and principles while thinking and acting in harmony with your highest aspirations.

*I*f you don't sell your time or use your time efficiently, then you simply cannot earn the kind of income that you want to earn.

*L*earn to love your work
and commit yourself to becoming
outstanding in your field.

You will have many ups and downs
in life, but what is most important
is that you remain true to yourself.
The starting point of developing a high level
of self-confidence is to think through and
decide upon your values.

*W*inners get there early,
they work late, they work through their lunch hour,
they work through their coffee breaks, they work
in the evenings, they study on the weekends,
they take extra courses. Winners are absolutely
determined to win, and they are willing
to pay the price.

*Take the time, pay any price,
do whatever is necessary to become the very
best at what you do.*

*B*ack every goal and plan
with persistent determination
and indomitable will power.

You can never really feel terrific about yourself, you can never really like yourself genuinely and accept yourself as a worthwhile person, until you have become good at what you do.

$\mathcal{T}$he reason why the vast majority of people are unhappy is that they are not good at anything. Every single human being has the ability to become good at something, so commit yourself to that, work at it, and pay any price to achieve that goal.

*Y*our level of persistence
in the face of adversity,
setbacks, and disappointments is your
exact measure of your belief in yourself.

The act of selecting your values is also the act of clearly stating to yourself exactly how you will live from this moment forward.

*C*ommit yourself to lifelong learning.
The most valuable asset you'll ever have is your
mind and what you put into it.

*T*he economic and personal results of individuals and corporations with clear values always tend to be far superior to those of companies and individuals whose values are vague or unclear.

*O*ne of the finest natural highs
is to choose a higher value and act on
that value no matter what the cost.
It will always turn out to be the right thing to do.

It is not what you say or hope or wish or intend but only what you do that counts. Your choices tell you unerringly who you really are.

*S*elf-confidence is a state of mind.
It is an attitude, and as an attitude
it is more important than facts.

The habit of setting and achieving ever-larger goals is absolutely indispensable to the development of ever-higher levels of strength and personal power.

*W*henever you violate or compromise your integrity, there seems to be a great power or force of retribution that will not allow you to get away with it.

If you are absolutely convinced
that you were meant to be a great success in life
and that there is nothing in the world that can stop
you from achieving great things as long as you persist,
you will become an irresistible force of nature.

$\mathcal{E}$ach time you write out your goals,
you drive them deeper into your subconscious mind;
you increase the intensity of your desire
and the depth of your belief.

*S*elf-confidence is the hinge upon which turns the gate of individual achievement.

*W*hatever you seem to enjoy the most is a very good indication of where your strengths lie.

*W*hen your self-confidence
becomes unlimited, you will be able to realize more
of your potential than you could under
any other circumstances.

*G*reat men and women are those who
absolutely believe that they are put
on earth to do something wonderful with their lives.

The depth of your belief and the strength of your conviction determine the power of your personality. If you really believe in your ability to succeed, you will become unstoppable.

When you truly believe yourself
to be an exceptional human being
who possesses remarkable capabilities,
you will walk and talk and act that way.

*G*oals will give you a clear sense
of direction and the knowledge
that your life is self-determined.

*T*here is no limit to what you can
accomplish if you know the direction you are going
and you are willing to make the effort.

*G*reat success is the result of countless hours, maybe even months and years, of preparation and hard work toward the goal of becoming very good at what you are doing.

*T*o develop unshakable self-confidence,
you need to see yourself and think of yourself
as a leader and do what leaders do.
You need to stretch yourself toward
the outermost boundaries of your potentials.

*A*ccepting responsibility is not an option that is open to the individual. It is mandatory. It is an absolute fact of human existence.

$\mathcal{I}$f you will consciously and deliberately give people what they want and need, they will reciprocate by giving you friendship, popularity, and a welcome wherever you go.

*A*n attitude of gratitude
enriches you in many ways.

*T*he world will largely accept you at your own
estimation. It is yourself that you have to convince
before you can convince anyone else.

*E*very positive, constructive action that you take in the direction of your dreams and goals will reinforce your belief in yourself and in your ability to accomplish your ideals.

*I*t is a fact of life that the more of yourself that you give away to others with no direct expectation of return, the more you will receive back, sometimes from the most unexpected sources.

When you develop the reputation of being a sincere listener, people will open up their hearts, their minds, and the doors of opportunity for you.

*P*eople from every walk of life
can dramatically increase their effectiveness
by building the trust and rapport
that only comes from good listening.

*A*pproach your life with
an attitude of positive expectancy.
Make the decision to remain calm, happy,
and positive no matter what happens.

*E*verything that you do to raise
the self-esteem of another person causes
your own self-esteem to go up.

*I*n order to be happy and to enjoy
high levels of self-confidence, you have to organize
your life in such a way that you feel very much
in control of what happens to you.

The critical measure of your physical health is your level of energy. The more energy you have, the more different things you can do and try and the more you will accomplish.

The quality of your entire personality
is affected by how you deal with adversity,
how well you keep your chin up.

*Y*ou feel positive about yourself to the degree to which you feel you are in control of your own life.

*W*hen you refuse to be pushed
or coerced into saying or doing something, you feel
much more in control of yourself and your life.

*Y*our peace of mind and personal satisfaction
are the most accurate guides you will
ever have to doing what is right for you.

People who genuinely like themselves
and accept themselves as valuable persons
like and accept other people to the same degree.

*S*trong people are those who dwell upon their strengths and abilities. Weak people are those who dwell upon their weaknesses and inabilities.

*Y*ou will never really be happy
or satisfied until you have found
a way to apply your unique human capabilities
to your life and to your work.

Sometimes you can defuse a difficult situation simply by being willing to understand the other person. Often all that people need is to know that someone else cares about how they feel and is attempting to understand their position.

The height to which you rise in life will always be determined by the depth of your own personal foundation, which is almost always the quality of your failures and what you have become as a result of them.

*D*iscontent and dissatisfaction almost always precede a constructive change that puts you onto the fast track and starts you growing.

*Y*our persistence is your measure of
your belief in yourself and your
ability to succeed.

*A*ll success is preceded by failure.

We can go no further in our evolution as human beings than we are at this moment, except by discarding our negative emotions.

*I*f you try enough different things in enough different ways and you learn from each trial, then you must inevitably be successful.

*E*verything that you do to improve
your physical well-being will have a positive impact
on how good you feel about yourself.

*E*verything you feel and all of your reactions are initially determined by how you think about any subject. If you change the quality of your thinking, you change the quality of your life.

When you reach the point where you believe in yourself absolutely, the barriers that exist in your external world will not stop you.
As soon as you win the inner battle, the outer battle seems to take care of itself.

Before falling asleep, think about the things you did right during the day and the things you are going to do better in the days to come. Soak your mind in positive images of yourself at your personal best.

*Y*our primary job is to make any effort, overcome any obstacle, and scale any height to become the dynamic, unstoppable, irresistibly self-confident person that you are capable of becoming.

*I*f you have the desire to change,
the decisiveness to take action, the determination
to persist on your forward track, and the discipline
to make yourself do whatever you need to do,
your self-confidence and your success are inevitable.

*B*y failing to plan, you plan to fail.

*T*he more often you dare to go forward,
even in the face of uncertainty, the more likely
it is that this type of courageous behavior will
become a habit for you.

*Y*ou are always free to choose. Everything you are and everything you become is under your own control.

*T*he feeling of personal fulfillment—the sense of self-actualization—is the hallmark of a truly mature, fully functioning human being.

For every effect in your life, there is a specific cause. If you don't like the effect you are experiencing, it is up to you to identify and change the causes.

You control your life by your thoughts.
If you wish your life to be different
in the future, you have to change your thinking
in the present.

We are continually acting as our own fortune-tellers by the way we talk to ourselves about how we think things will turn out in our lives.

The key to success is to take full control of the conscious mind and to keep your conscious mind totally on what you want to accomplish.

Your level of adherence to the values you have personally selected is the real measure of your quality as a human being.

$\mathcal{E}$verything you do to improve the quality of your thinking must, by extension, improve the quality of your life.

$\mathcal{A}$ thought without a feeling does not generate a reaction in our lives. A feeling without a thought does not generate a direction. So, thought and feeling must be mixed.

$\mathcal{M}$ake your life a total affirmation.
From the time you get up in the morning, remember
that everything that you think about is having an effect
on the person that you are becoming.

*A*s long as you know that you are living a life consistent with your highest principles, your self-confidence rests on an unshakable foundation.

$\mathcal{Y}$ou are continually evolving and growing toward the realization of your ideal self. The more clear that ideal self is in your imagination, the more rapidly you become that person.

*A*s long as you keep your mind clearly focused on the goal that you want to accomplish, you will achieve that goal.

The more you can develop an absolute conviction, a complete faith in your ability to achieve your goal, the more rapidly you move toward its attainment.

*G*oals are what make us stretch.
They cause us to move out of
our comfort zone and operate on the outer
edge of our potential as human beings,
so make your goals challenging.

*Y*our major definite purpose
in life should always be measurable,
specific, and quantifiable.

*S*elf-discipline is persistence in action.

*P*ositive thinkers think and talk continually about solutions, and negative thinkers continually talk and think about problems. Keep your mind solution-focused rather than problem-focused.

The more clear and precise your goals can be and the more committed you are to accomplishing them, the more rapidly your capabilities will work to impel and project those goals into your life.

*Y*our persistence is the direct measure
of how much you believe in yourself
and in your ability to succeed.

*T*he surest way to get other people to be
interested in you is to be interested in them.

*W*e never achieve happiness by going out and trying to become happy. We only achieve happiness by engaging on a day-to-day basis in activities that we find valuable and worthwhile.

*T*he tendency to look for the good
in every situation is a direct measure of how
healthy your personality is.

*I*f it were not for the fear of rejection,
we would all be terrific sales people.

*O*ngoing commitment to personal and professional development gives you a feeling of continuous growth.

*Y*ou are not what you think you are; but what you think, you are.

*Y*ou have a healthy personality to the degree to which you can get along with the greatest number of different types of people.

*D*ecide exactly what it is you want in life, set it as a goal, and decide the price you are going to have to pay to get it. Remember, nothing worthwhile ever came without sacrifice.

The illiterate is the person who
is no longer learning and growing and
increasing his or her value every single day.

ut your whole heart and soul into
your success. Don't hold anything back and
don't let anything stop you or discourage you.

The key question to time management is, What is the most valuable use of my time right now?

You only learn how to succeed by failing, and no success is possible without it.

*G*uard your integrity as a sacred thing.
Be true to yourself and to your own goals.

*W*hen you see a problem or an
obstacle, always look upon it as a challenge.

*E*verybody has the ability to do at least
one thing, and sometimes more than one thing,
in an outstanding fashion. What holds us back is the
belief that we are just average, that we really don't
have the ability so what's the use in trying.

*W*ith greater self-confidence you can deal more effectively with the inevitable problems and difficulties that arise in day-to-day life. You will think continually in terms of solutions and how you can turn any situation to your best advantage.

*C*ontinually making excuses and trying to explain away your faults, your problems, and your deficiencies, instead of accepting full responsibility for your life and doing something to change it, is one of the critical factors that can hold you back from achieving your full potential as a human being.

*E*very person is put on this earth with a unique combination of ingredients that make him or her different from anyone else. It is when you find the situation that can most benefit your special capabilities that you will be able to make the greatest contribution and enjoy the greatest rewards, both tangible and intangible.

*Y*our thought is the most powerful force in your universe. It is both creative and causative—every minute of every day it is forming the world around you.

*Y*our ability to succeed in your closest personal relationships affects your self-confidence in every other part of your life.

*M*oney doesn't come quickly and easily,
it comes only with persistent hard work
done continuously over an extended period of time.
There is no easy way to become successful.